Congratulations!

Your search for the ***ideal journal*** that meets your ***"needs and requirements"*** *is over.*

The following dot-formatted pages will give you the flexibility of customizing your notebook into anything and everything you want it to be according to your own ***"unique personality and lifestyle."***

- Planner
- Diary
- Sketchbook
- Calendar
- Log and List
- Scheduler
- Coloring Book
- Story Book
- Music Book
- Project Progress Chart
- Scrapbook
- Photo Album
- Activity Book
- and more!

The sky is the limit to what you can do. Take it as far as your creative imagination leads you.

It is after all your own **DIY** book. So go ahead and utilize it anyhow that makes sense and gives **JOY** to you and only **YOU**.

Bring out your washi tape, gel pens, and clippings and start planning your next big adventure, logging your dreams and tracking your savings with your own spread, planner, illustrations, vision pages and more that truly reflect your true self.

Have F-U-N!

Happy Bullet Journaling*!*

This Journal belongs to

____

This beginner friendly Bullet Journaling paper includes:
12 BONUS Pages for reference to get your creative juices flowing into a joyful grid paper journaling experience:

150+ bullet journaling ideas under 15 categories
15 logs and chart samples
planner samples
font samples
150+ sample elements (motifs, banners, etc.)
and has (is):

- 9"L x 6"W dimensions
  (small enough for the purse and to carry around/roomy enough for your custom made entries)
- 172 pages (includes page for Owner's name and 12 Bonus pages-see above)
- 150 dotted grid paper (.2" distance space between dots)
- 0.00225" (0.0572 mm) paper thickness
  (perfect for light coloring-ideal for use with gel pens, crayons, colored pencils)
- White paper- Perfect bound
- Attractive Soft Glossy Cover
- (various titles available in different sizes, matte cover and cream paper)

Find us on Amazon and check our growing selection from **"Journals by Victoria"** from planners, notebooks, activity books, trackers and other low content books and find your favorite. They make for delightful present for Birthdays and Graduations, Get well and Christmas.

- 2019: The best is yet to come (ISBN: 978-1728787152)
- Always be Wondering (ISBN: 978-1725107670)
- Always be Wondering (ISBN: 978-1726878678)
- Be as Happy as You can be (ISBN: 978-1724877055)
- Be as Happy as You can be (ISBN: 978-1728723662)
- Be still and know (ISBN: 978-1728779812)
- Be still and know (ISBN: 978-1728778396)
- Be still and know (ISBN: 978-1728779508
- Count your Blessings not your Troubles (ISBN: 978-1726797498)
- Dare to be Different (ISBN: 978-1728783611)
- Dot Journal for Newbies: Festival (ISBN: 978-1728742403)
- Give Thanks (ISBN: 978-1728743738)
- Give Thanks (ISBN: 978-1728743578)
- Happy Camper (ISBN: 978-1728722837)
- Home is where good coffee is (ISBN: 978-1728780511)
- I may live in the Midwest…Hollywood (ISBN: 978-172874203)
- Let your ideas bloom (ISBN: 978-1728781198)
- Let your ideas bloom (ISBN: 978-1728781198)
- Life is better on a boat (ISBN: 978-1724878809)
- Never lose your Sparkle (ISBN: 978-1726849920)
- One step at a time (ISBN: 978-1728743059)
- Silence is better than Bullshit (ISBN: 978-1728788135)
- Strive for Progress Not Perfection (ISBN:978-1726795074)
- And more…!!!

*We appreciate your feedback and suggestions by leaving a review on Amazon… **thank you very much!***

Ideas for the Bullet Journal Newbie

Trackers:
- Mood Trackers
- Food Tracker
- Fitness Tracker
- Mental Health Tracker
- 21-day New Habit Progress
- Expense Tracker

Collections
- Future Log
- Master Wish List
- Birthdays
- Gift Ideas
- Yearly Goals
- Master-to-do-List
- Coins found everywhere

Finances and Money
- Savings Tracker
- Credit Card Debt Tracker
- Student Loan Repayment
- Income Streams
- Monthly Bills
- No-spend Challenge
- Car Payment Tracker
- Coupon websites
- Discount Sites and Offers

Business
- Business Expense/Mileage
- Company Parties/Conferences
- Hours Worked
- Incidents and Issues Record
- Projects, Promotions ,Certificates
- Trainings

Family
- Family Date Night Ideas
- Memories
- Last time I called
- Recipes to try
- Pet/Vet Tracker
- Emergency Contact Numbers

Entertainment
- Books to Read
- Movies to Watch
- Songs to Download
- Crafts Ideas
- TV shows to Watch
- TV Shoe episode/Season tracker
- Movie Release Dates
- Party Ideas
- Liquor Cabinet Inventory

Children and Kids
- Funny Things my kids say
- Milestones
- Behavior and Trigger Tracker
- Kid's Birthday/Christmas Wish List
- Dentist/Doctor's Appointments
- Last time kids got Haircut
- Kids Crafty Ideas
- Indoor Activities for Kids
- School/Day care Contact info
- Allergy and Care Info
- Chores/Tasks Assignment
- School Activities Schedule
- Baby Name List
- Dedicated child specific date   ideas

Home and Household
- Weekly/Monthly Cleaning Schedule
- Big Cleanout Projects
- Yard Sale Ideas
- Yard Sale Inventory/Ideas
- Renovation/Upgrade Ideas/Budget
- Home Items Wish List/Need to Buy
- Master Grocery List
- Vehicle Maintenance Schedule/Record
- Freezer Inventory
- Borrowed/Returned Tracker

Relationships
- Yearly Relationship Goals
- Sex Tracker
- Date Tracker/Log
- Favorite Memories
- Things to do for/with
- Things we argue about
- Husband/Wife's Interest
- Wedding Planner

Social Media
- Blogging Ideas
- Monthly Page Views
- Sponsored Post Opportunities
- Blogging /You tube Income
- Facebook Groups and Pages
- Friends /Linked Parties
- Common Friends with
- Guest Post Opportunities
- Websites to submit content to
- Affiliates Marketing
- Record/Opportunities
- Ad companies and Income
- Posting Schedule
- Password Log
- Multi Social Media following/fans log

Self-care Wellness

Gratitude Log
Daily Act of Kindness
My favorite things
Things to do before I die
Things that make me Happy
Anxiety Attack /Trigger tracker
Things that make me feel
Medications
Living my Best Life tracker
Inspirational Quotes
Prayer Log
Affirmations
Skills to Learn
Dream Tracker
Steps to Relax
Products I Love
Employment History
Wardrobe Tracker
Fashion Ideas to try

Hobbies

Things to try
Hobbies Schedule
Skills Level and Progress
New Hobby Progress Chart
Local associations addresses
Hobbies Convention/Cost
Hobbies Gadgets Inventory
Hobbies Cost Tracker
Hobbies Income Potential
Hobbies Match with friends

School

Schedule
Test Days
Parent/Teachers Contacts List
Grades Tracker
Study Techniques
Classmates/Teachers birthday list

Travel

Places I have been
Travel Bucket List
Packing Checklist
Hotels I like/Reviews
Things to do in ____________
Pre-vacation Checklist
Flight Miles Log
Camping Checklist/Inventory
Favorite Places to camp
Favorite places to eat
Road trip Planner

Health and Fitness

Workout Log
Clean eating meal and snacks ideas
30-day fitness challenge
Yoga sequences
Weight loss Tracker
Inches lost tracker
Rewards for reaching goals
Things to do instead of snack
Walking distance/Steps tacker
Calorie/Meal tracker
Home workout Ideas
Period/Ovulation Tracker

Daily Good Deed / Random Act of Kindness

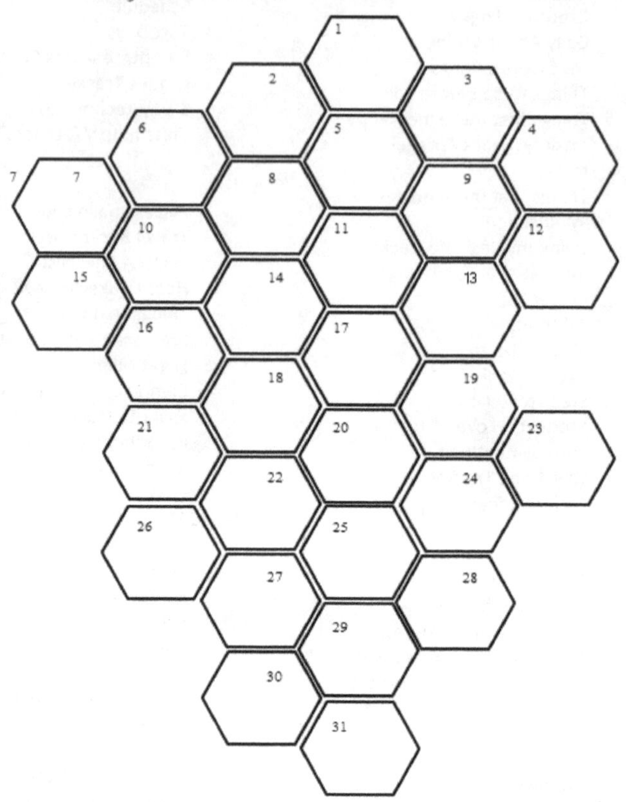

Weekly Schedule

6 Monday			
7 Tuesday			
8 Wednesday			
9 Thursday			
10 Friday			
11 Saturday			
12 Sunday			

<table>
<tr><td colspan="2">

TO DO
* _______________
* _______________
* _______________
* _______________
* _______________
* _______________
* _______________
* _______________
* _______________
* _______________
* _______________
* _______________
* _______________

</td><td>

F O C U S

</td><td>

7:00 AM ____
8:00 AM ____
9:00 AM ____
10:00 AM ____
11:00 AM ____
12:00 PM ____
1:00 PM ____
2:00 PM ____
3:00 PM ____
4:00 PM ____
5:00 PM ____
6:00 PM ____
7:00 PM ____
8:00 PM ____
9:00 PM ____
10:00 PM ____
11:00 PM ____

</td></tr>
</table>

9:00 PM
8:00 PM
7:00 PM
6:00 PM
5:00 PM
4:00 PM
3:00 PM
2:00 PM
1:00 PM
12:00 PM
11:00 AM
10:00 AM
9:00 AM
8:00 AM

1 2 3 4 5 6 7 8 9 10 11 ≥ 1 oz

Today's Word

Grateful for

NOTES

Dream Log

Date: ___________

Place of Dream

People in the Dream

What happened in the Dream

Notes: _________________________
____
____

Nutrition / Health and Wellness

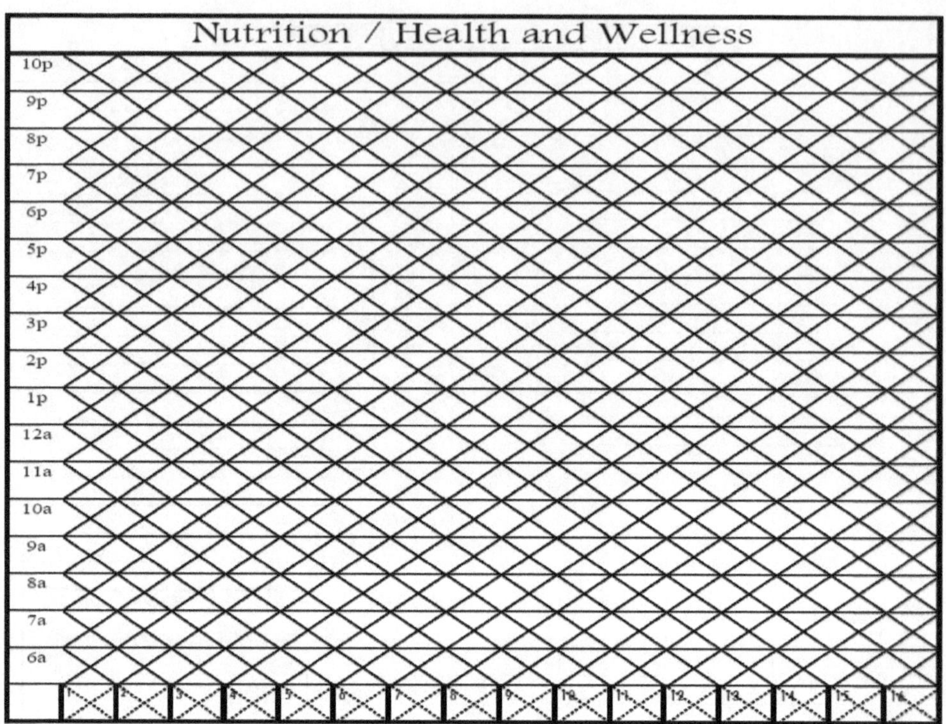

	Legend							
Items	**Color Code**	**1 unit**	**Symbols**				**Daily Goal**	**End of Day**
Fruits	Orange	/cup	☆					
Vegetables	Green	/serve	◯					
Carbs	Silver	/serve						
Calories	Orange	/serve	♡					
Steps/Walk	Grey	/25 steps	△					
Workout	Red	/25 min						
Sleep	Pink	/hr.						
Water	Blue	/oz.						

Daily Expense Log

Items	Price	Balance
End of Day		$

Nutrition Health and Fitness Tracker

	1	2	3	4	5	6	7	8	9	10	11	12
10p												
9p												
8p												
7p												
6p												
5p												
4p												
3p												
2p												
1p												
12a												
11a												
10a												
9a												
8a												
7a												
6a												

Birthday List

	JAN	FEB	MAR	APR	MAY	JUNE	JUL	AUG	SEPT	OCT	NOV	DEC
1												
2												
3												
4												
5												
6												
7												
8												
9												
10												
11												
12												
13												
14												
15												

Week of _______________________________

Monday

Tuesday

Wednesday

Thursday

Friday

Saturday

Sunday

MONTHLY MOOD TRACKER

	Morning	Afternoon	Evening
1			
2			
3			
4			
5			
6			
7			
8			
9			
10			
11			
12			
13			
14			
15			
16			
17			
18			
19			
20			
21			
22			
23			
24			
25			
26			
27			
28			
29			
30			
31			

Moods	
Silver	Calm
Baby Blue	Gullible
Blue	Confident
Pink	Sweet
Fuschia	Bold
Lavander	Royal
Purple	Artistic
Orange	Bold
Grey	Doubtful
Black	Grieving
Yelllow	Happy
Aqua	
Mint Gree	
Red	Angry
	Suspicious
	Despressed
	Hopeful

Living my Best Balanced Life

Annual Goals Chart

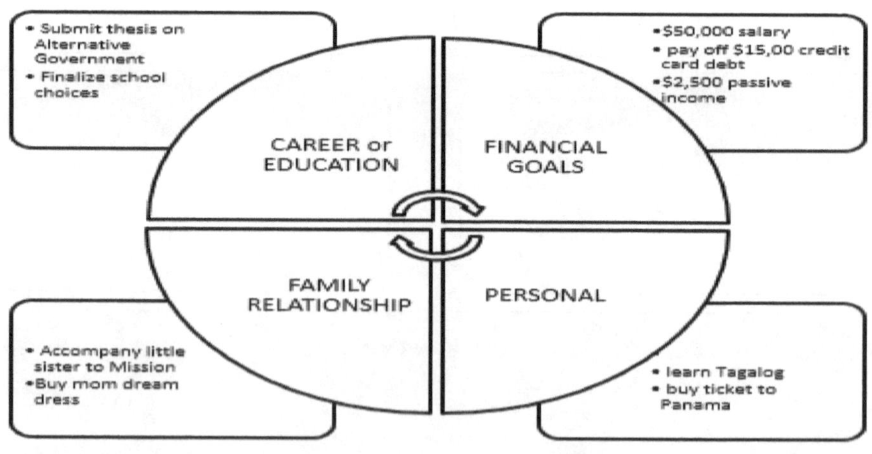

Monday	WORD OF THE WEEK	Tuesday

Goals for the Week

| Wednesday | | Thursday |

| Friday | Expense Tracker
Item __ /$ | Saturday |

| Sunday | Workout/Gym Tracker Total | Next Week |

Date

" Today I am________________________ "
" Today I feel_______________________ "

TO DO		Time		Status
		6:00 AM		
		7:00 AM		
		8:00 AM		
		9:00 AM		
		10:00 AM		
		11:00 AM		
		12:00 PM		
		1:00 PM		
		2:00 PM		
		3:00 PM		
		4:00 PM		
To Buy		5:00 PM		
		6:00 PM		
		7:00 PM		
		8:00 PM		
		9:00 PM		
		10:00 PM		

Act of Kindness   Act of Self-love   Grateful for

Expense Log		
Item	Debit/Credit	Balance
Total	$	

MUST DO FOR TOMORROW

End of Day's Notes

ACTIVITY PROGRESS CHART
Knitting Project #1   Red Scarf

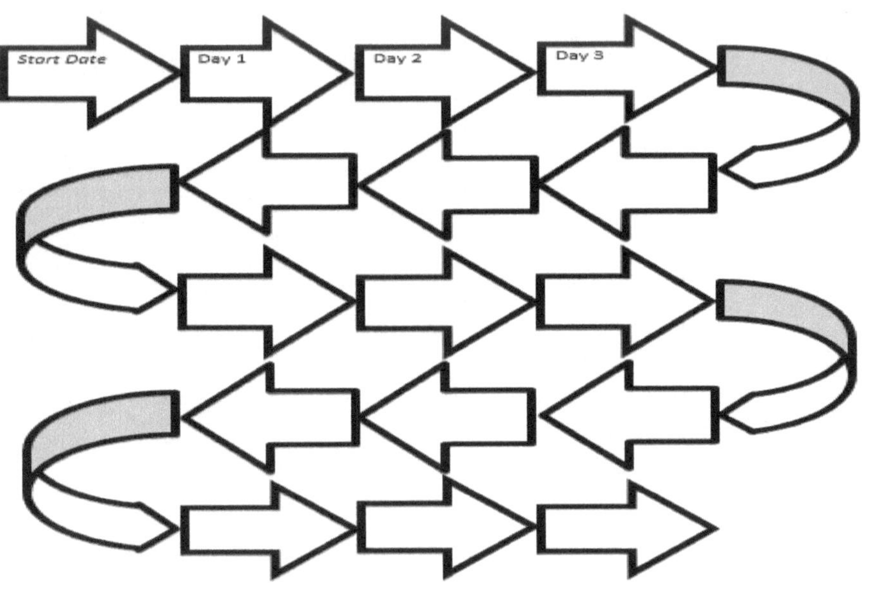

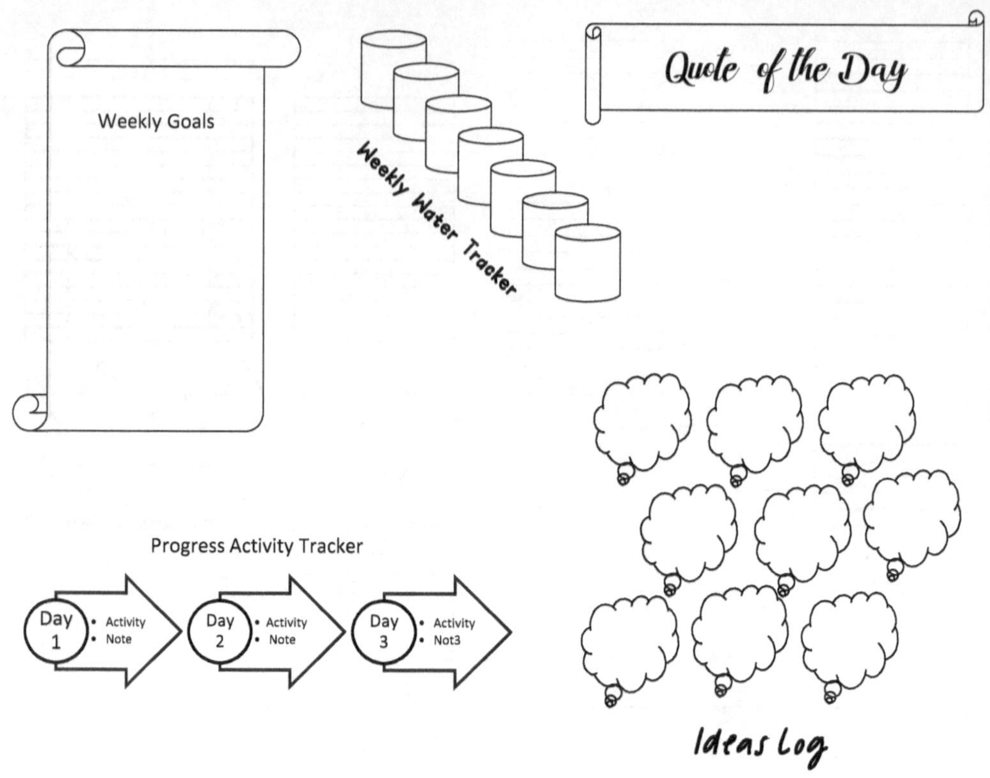

Sleep Log

	1	2	3	4	5	6	7	8	9	10	11	12	13	14	15	16	17	18	19	20	21	22	23	24
1	1	2	3	4	5	6	7	8	9	10	11	12	13	14	15	16	17	18	19	20	21	22	23	24
2	1	2	3	4	5	6	7	8	9	10	11	12	13	14	15	16	17	18	19	20	21	22	23	24
3	1	2	3	4	5	6	7	8	9	10	11	12	13	14	15	16	17	18	19	20	21	22	23	24
4	1	2	3	4	5	6	7	8	9	10	11	12	13	14	15	16	17	18	19	20	21	22	23	24
5	1	2	3	4	5	6	7	8	9	10	11	12	13	14	15	16	17	18	19	20	21	22	23	24
6	1	2	3	4	5	6	7	8	9	10	11	12	13	14	15	16	17	18	19	20	21	22	23	24
7	1	2	3	4	5	6	7	8	9	10	11	12	13	14	15	16	17	18	19	20	21	22	23	24
8	1	2	3	4	5	6	7	8	9	10	11	12	13	14	15	16	17	18	19	20	21	22	23	24
9	1	2	3	4	5	6	7	8	9	10	11	12	13	14	15	16	17	18	19	20	21	22	23	24
10	1	2	3	4	5	6	7	8	9	10	11	12	13	14	15	16	17	18	19	20	21	22	23	24
11	1	2	3	4	5	6	7	8	9	10	11	12	13	14	15	16	17	18	19	20	21	22	23	24
12	1	2	3	4	5	6	7	8	9	10	11	12	13	14	15	16	17	18	19	20	21	22	23	24
13	1	2	3	4	5	6	7	8	9	10	11	12	13	14	15	16	17	18	19	20	21	22	23	24
14	1	2	3	4	5	6	7	8	9	10	11	12	13	14	15	16	17	18	19	20	21	22	23	24
15	1	2	3	4	5	6	7	8	9	10	11	12	13	14	15	16	17	18	19	20	21	22	23	24
16	1	2	3	4	5	6	7	8	9	10	11	12	13	14	15	16	17	18	19	20	21	22	23	24
17	1	2	3	4	5	6	7	8	9	10	11	12	13	14	15	16	17	18	19	20	21	22	23	24
18	1	2	3	4	5	6	7	8	9	10	11	12	13	14	15	16	17	18	19	20	21	22	23	24
19	1	2	3	4	5	6	7	8	9	10	11	12	13	14	15	16	17	18	19	20	21	22	23	24
20	1	2	3	4	5	6	7	8	9	10	11	12	13	14	15	16	17	18	19	20	21	22	23	24
21	1	2	3	4	5	6	7	8	9	10	11	12	13	14	15	16	17	18	19	20	21	22	23	24
22	1	2	3	4	5	6	7	8	9	10	11	12	13	14	15	16	17	18	19	20	21	22	23	24
23	1	2	3	4	5	6	7	8	9	10	11	12	13	14	15	16	17	18	19	20	21	22	23	24
24	1	2	3	4	5	6	7	8	9	10	11	12	13	14	15	16	17	18	19	20	21	22	23	24
25	1	2	3	4	5	6	7	8	9	10	11	12	13	14	15	16	17	18	19	20	21	22	23	24
26	1	2	3	4	5	6	7	8	9	10	11	12	13	14	15	16	17	18	19	20	21	22	23	24
27	1	2	3	4	5	6	7	8	9	10	11	12	13	14	15	16	17	18	19	20	21	22	23	24
28	1	2	3	4	5	6	7	8	9	10	11	12	13	14	15	16	17	18	19	20	21	22	23	24
29	1	2	3	4	5	6	7	8	9	10	11	12	13	14	15	16	17	18	19	20	21	22	23	24
30	1	2	3	4	5	6	7	8	9	10	11	12	13	14	15	16	17	18	19	20	21	22	23	24
31	1	2	3	4	5	6	7	8	9	10	11	12	13	14	15	16	17	18	19	20	21	22	23	24

Good Morning

GOOD MORNING

Good Morning

Good Morning

GOOD MORNING

GOOD MORNING

GOOD MORNING

Good Morning

Good Morning

GOOD MORNING

GOOD morning

Good Morning

GOOD MORNING

GOOD MORNING

Good Morning

GOOD MORNING

Good Morning

Good Morning

Good Morning

Good Morning

Good Morning

Good Morning

Good Morning

GOOD MORNING

GOOD MORNING

GOOD MORNING

Good Morning

GOOD MORNING

Good Morning

Good Morning

Good Morning

Good Morning

GOOD MORNING

Good Morning

GOOD MORNING

Good Morning

Good Morning

Good Morning

Good Morning

GOOD MORNING

Good Morning

GOOD MORNING

GOOD MORNING

Good Morning

Good Morning

Good Morning

Good Morning

Good Morning

Good Morning

Good Morning

GOOD MORNING

GOOD MORNING

Good Morning

GOOD MORNING

YOU CAN'T SCARE ME
Wild One
LIFE'S A GARDEN DIG IT
I want shoes
I WANT SHOES
I want shoes
GOSH
Being a Princess IS EXHAUSTING!
& Muscles Mascara
SWEET, SASSY & SOUTHERN

EVEN UNICORNS
NEED COFFEE
meh.
TGIF! Yes!
Happiness is believing in unicorns
difficult ROADS lead To beautiful destionations
Be happy
Cheers!
I CAN'T adult TODAY
MAKE your OWN magic
THE best IS YET TO come
NAMAST'AY in bed
Gratitude
YOU ARE enough
Road trip warrior
Crafting is happiness
Start THE DAY WITH A Smile
Be Brave
Be free
Let the journey begin
Plant Dreams pull Weeds & grow a Happy Life
Girl Boss
Seize the Day
follow YOUR heart
QUEEN OF ROAD TRIPS
Good Times
YOUR vibe Attracts your tribe
Be The Reason Someone SMILES
FOLLOW YOUR CURIOSITY
MAMA'S little MIRACLE